Table of Contents

Chapter 1: Advice for Students

*"The most stressful part about choosing a career
~ is simply making a choice."*

There is a time in high school when students start to seriously think about choosing a career path. Of course, there are always individuals that, from very early on, are drawn toward a specific calling and will never know the struggle of deciding what to focus on in life. However, choosing a career path and making a definitive decision places an immense amount of pressure on the majority of young students.

What you want to be when you grow up requires some serious thought. The pressure to get decent grades – and the fact that grades heavily influence what one can and cannot do – results in many students making scattered, hurried, and uneducated decisions.

There is also the added pressure of having to qualify for a career you're not quite sure you will like and will have to wait four to seven years to get.

During this time, the realization may also set in that you don't possess the fire in your belly like others do, and it may frustrate and disappoint you that you can't identify your true calling. This is especially the case if you are experiencing any added pressure from family, friends, the education system, or even from our fear-of-failure culture.

Perhaps internally you feel like any indecisiveness and confusion about choosing a career path will be considered as a disappointment to those you care about. This can be difficult to cope with, and can often result in a hasty career choice just to make others happy.

So, what to do?

Instead of becoming heavily burdened and disheartened by the fact that you're not locked into a desirable career trajectory, let's try focusing on the **process** of career selection - instead of merely career selecting.

This book will gently guide you down a road of self-discovery and help you become aware of your true potential.

Remember that every single person on this planet is their own unique individual and has their own unique gift - their own 'light' - to offer this world. Keep this in mind so as to make the best decision *for yourself*, not what others may think is best for you.

We hope the information offered in the next few chapters will resonate with you and spur you in the direction that you are meant to go in. The effects of self-discovery may include clarity, happiness, and fulfillment!

"I can not do everything, but I can do something. I must not fail to do the something that I can do."

~ Helen Keller

Chapter 2: Start Thinking Early

"Choose a job you love, and you will never have to work a day in your life."

~ Confucius

Figuring out what you want to be doing for the rest of your life can seem like a daunting, almost impossible task. And the more choices you have, the more anxiety it can cause and the more fear you can have of making the wrong decision.

If you are still in high school, one of the most beneficial things you can do is to think about what you may like to do (and not like to do) as early on as possible - the more time to learn about and consider all the options available to you, the better.

Research a few targeted career options that you think you may like and put your energy into that instead of pigeonholing yourself into one particular career path and gambling that it's the right choice.

Take your time and learn about potential careers in depth by reading books or by looking up information on the internet. When you are reading about a certain career, imagine yourself going through the motions of that career, and being in that type of work environment.

Many students may start thinking about going down a certain career path based on what subjects they get high grades in, what they like to do in their spare time, or what a relative or parent does for a living.

For example, a student that excels in math may decide to become an engineer or an accountant, a student that is good in English may decide to go in the direction of journalism or communications, or someone interested in hair, make-up or fashion may think of becoming a hairdresser, a make-up artist, or a fashion designer.

You may also see children follow in their parent's footsteps. For example, if a parent or grandparent has a family business, or is a lawyer or doctor, the child may decide that this is a suitable career path for them to take as well.

As a first step when thinking about careers, it's definitely good to jot down a few careers that you think may align with your strengths and/or likes, and to even jot down some 'maybe' careers you're not sure of.

However, a word of caution at this point. Just because you like doing certain things, have gotten good grades in a particular subject, or think it might be a good idea to follow in your parent's footsteps - **doesn't mean that you will be well-suited to do the job, or that you would find the job enjoyable.**

If you choose a career that is not suitable for you, or if the job involves working in an environment that makes you feel uncomfortable, you could be stuck in a career like a round pin in a square hole. This is best avoided, as disillusionment can seep in very quickly once the realization hits that a career doesn't mesh well with your personality and interests.

Information Gathering Interviews

A helpful suggestion during career hunting is to not only gather information from books and the internet, but to get information about a field of work from someone who has some firsthand knowledge. You can ask anyone as long as that person is knowledgeable about the area in which you are interested.

Ask your teachers, friends, neighbours, or relatives if they know someone you can talk to and 'interview'. People love to talk about what they do and you may be pleasantly surprised at how open they can be to meet with you. You could even call or email someone you have read about and who has your "dream job". Ask if you can take a few minutes of their time to ask them some questions about what they do. Also, make a point of letting them know that you are looking for information only, not a job.

An example of how you could phrase your request is: "Would it be possible to schedule a meeting with you at your convenience to ask a few questions and get your advice on how I can best prepare to enter the field? I promise to not take more than 20-30 minutes of your time."

Make sure you research the career of interest so you are able to ask intelligent questions and not waste the person's time. The information gathering interview is an excellent way to get an idea if the career may be a good fit for you, so take time to think about the questions you want answers to. Here are a few questions you may want to ask:

Could you describe a typical day at work?

What type of person is a good fit for this career?

How many hours/week do you work? Is there overtime/weekend work involved?

Do you see this field growing in the future?

What is the advancement potential in the field? What is a typical path?

What do you like and what don't you like about this career?

What do you wish someone had told you about this career before you got into it?

If you could start all over again, would you change your career path in any way? Why?

What advice would you give to someone looking to get into this field of work?

Is there anything else you think I need to know?

It's a really nice gesture to follow up with a thank-you note within one to two days thanking the person for their time and for the information they freely gave you. This can be sent by way of email or business letter. If you had a nice interaction with the person, keep in touch by letting him or her know how things are going with you and expressing how their advice has been helpful.

"I am not a product of my circumstances. I am a product of my decisions."

~ Stephen Covey

Chapter 3: Who Am I As a Person?

We ask ourselves, 'Who am I to be brilliant, gorgeous, talented, fabulous?'
Actually, who are you not to be?

~ Marianne Williamson

"Who am I?" is probably one of the most interesting, overwhelming and difficult questions you can ask yourself. It seems like such a simple question, yet it can leave you feeling perplexed and even embarrassed that you don't have a clear and concise answer.

"Who am I?" is a difficult question because it takes some self-observation and soul-searching to answer it. This is to be expected since we are all complex beings.

You do not get to know yourself just because you have grown up or have grown old. Getting to know yourself takes conscious effort; and you need to do it with intention and with purpose. By stopping and taking a bit of time to explore who you are and what makes you unique, you will be able to open the door to your inner self and discover what lane you should be travelling on. This is especially important when it comes to determining your career direction.

Try taking some time to get to know what your skill sets, your passions, your personality, and your values are. Deciding on a career direction will then become a lot clearer to you.

Knowing yourself well and knowing what makes you tick is key to making the best decisions about your future. If you're in school, you may have some big influences, such as your parents and/or teachers, that are nudging (or even pushing) you towards a certain career. However, that direction may not really be suited to who you are and to what will ultimately make you happy.

The key to getting to know who you are is to ask yourself some introspective questions. The process is no different than earnestly wanting to get to know someone else - you ask meaningful questions and receive honest answers that begin to paint a picture of who that person really is.

These questions may seem fairly simple at first glance, however once you really start thinking about them and honestly answering them, you may discover some interesting things about yourself that you hadn't thought of before.

Your answers will start to point you in the direction of finding a career that will make you feel happy and fulfilled. Everything you experience in life flows from how well you know yourself.

If you have a difficult time answering any of the questions, ask friends and family to help you out. Sometimes those close to us are able to pinpoint things about our personality better than we can.

Ok, it's time to get out a piece of paper and a pen and jot down your answers to the following questions:

What activities make me happy?

Do you like writing, helping other people, working with your hands, or learning how to program on the computer? Perhaps you like being with and taking care of animals, playing a musical instrument, or learning about other countries and cultures.

Am I more cooperative or competitive?

How you view your cooperative versus competitive tendencies is very important when thinking about a career choice.

What am I doing when I'm in flow?

There may be a certain activity you do that will make the time just fly by. When you lose all track of time, you are in a state of 'flow'. Pay attention to what you are doing when this happens, as this will give you a big clue as to what you truly love to do and what avenue you may want to pursue.

What if money wasn't a consideration?

If you didn't need to worry about money for food and housing in your life, how would you spend your time? Would you volunteer for a certain cause? Would you dive into a particular hobby? Would you think about starting your own company? Would you spend your time travelling?

Am I more of a 'thinker' or a 'doer'?

Do you have concepts and ideas in your head but are hesitant to actually put those ideas into effect? or are you more of a driven and determined type of person that is willing to take a chance on things?

Do I consider myself to be an artistic, creative person, or am I more interested in routine, concrete activities?

Some people are amazing at partaking in their own creative abilities, and others are merely great at appreciating the talents of others. Which one do you relate to most?

By taking the time to think these through and answer these questions honestly, you are forming a stronger sense of self-awareness. Here are a few more questions to ask yourself. Remember to be completely honest when answering, as there are no right or wrong answers:

If you were to describe a perfect day, what would it look like?

How would you spend the rest of your time on earth if you only had six months to live?

Are you happy? If not, what would make you happy?

Have you been dishonest with other people or yourself? About what? Why?

What do you wish people would say about you at your funeral?

What's missing from your life? What do you think you can you do to get it?

Are there certain areas of your life where you are underestimating yourself?

What gifts, talents, or passions have you been hiding from yourself and the world? Are these things you can incorporate into your life and career? How?

When you know yourself you are empowered. When you accept yourself you are invincible.

-- Tina Lifford

In the following chapters, we will address certain questions and topics in greater depth. As you go through each chapter, make sure to write down your answers to any questions and to take notes on things you read that strike a deep cord within you. The ways you react, whether in positive or negative ways, are all clues as to what will ultimately make you happy and fulfilled in your future.

Chapter 4: What Type of Environment Do I See Myself In?

"Your outlook upon life, your estimate of yourself, your estimate of your value are largely colored by your environment. Your whole career will be modified, shaped, molded by your surroundings, by the character of the people with whom you come in contact every day."

~ Orison Swett Marden

Asking yourself questions is a great way to step into self-discovery and personal growth. Your answers to the following questions will shed some light as to what type of environment you feel most comfortable in.

Should I Work Indoors?

The obvious benefit to being indoors is protection against the elements - rain, snow, wind and sun. Working indoors may also involve sitting behind a desk, standing for long periods, being under fluorescent lights, and breathing in limited fresh air.

While this may not appeal to everyone, it does appeal to those who prefer a stable and predictable type of environment.

Accountants, librarians, aestheticians, doctors, nurses, administrative assistants, bankers, writers, lawyers, professors, computer engineers, etc., are all examples of people that have chosen careers that have indoor environments.

These jobs may at times involve traveling to other offices or buildings or even involve travelling to other states or countries, however, for the most part, they exclude working outside for a large part of the work day.

Should I Work Outdoors?

If the thought of a nine-to-five office job fills you with dread, and would much prefer to be connected to nature rather than to a desk, then working outdoors may be more suitable for you.

Archaeologists, surveyors, ski instructors, construction workers, forest rangers, journalists, police officers, marine biologists, horse trainers, travel guides etc., are all examples of people that have chosen careers that involve outdoor environments.

People in these careers prefer being active and have a more adventurous personality. They feel very connected to nature and/or the feeling of freedom, and don't mind being exposed to bugs, animals, unpredictable weather conditions, and at times dangerous situations.

If you love being outside then having an indoor job will only frustrate you, and likewise, if you love being inside then having an outdoor job will be just awful for you. Deciding what your preference is will further hone your career search.

Do I Like People in My Environment?

This may seem like a strange question, however knowing how you feel when you're with other people is very important when trying to choose a career.

How comfortable do you feel when you are in a room full of people?

How do you feel when you have to interact with people?

How comfortable do you feel when you are alone?

Do you feel exhausted when you have to collaborate with others or have to make small talk?

Knowing what type of 'people environment' you prefer can help steer you towards a certain career direction.

If you regularly hear those close to you describing you as friendly, outgoing, or the life of the party, you are most likely a people person. If you truly love being around others and get your energy from external influences, it would be ideal to be able to incorporate your extroverted personality into your career.

There are many career choices out there that require people skills. A few examples include motivational speaker, personal trainer, physician, nurse, teacher, flight attendant, counselor, life coach, sales manager, hairdresser, choreographer, actor, receptionist, entrepreneur, etc.

On the other hand, if you prefer your own space and being with just a few people instead of a crowd, you may be more on the introverted side. You may like to listen and observe rather than get up and speak in front of an audience, and may prefer to work with little or no supervision.

Introversion is not a negative thing, and as many of the best careers for introverts prove, having this type of personality can become a big asset. A few career examples include private chef, animal trainer, welder, lab technician, mechanic, engineer, statistician, editor, pilot, writer, astronomer, physicist, computer programmer, etc.

What Type of Workplace Environment Do I Want?

There are hundreds if not thousands of careers that one can pick from. Some require you to work in a 'standard' type of workplace environment - for example, receptionists, nurses and teachers work in offices, hospitals, and schools.

However, there are careers that will have you travelling to new cities, states, and even countries on a regular basis. Such is the case for journalists, wildlife photographers, flight attendants and pilots.

Determine if you would prefer a stable workplace, or a career that will allow you to discover new places and meet new people.

If you don't think you're suited for a career that needs you to get up and go as needed, then you can rule out the careers requiring a lot of travel.

What Kind of 'Responsibility Environment' Do I Want?

It's important to determine the amount of responsibility you think you'd be comfortable with in your career - as your level of happiness may be affected if it's too much or too little.

For example, there are people who prefer to be responsible for one project at a time, working until completion before moving on to the next. They are more methodical in their approach, and prefer to do things carefully, thoroughly, and in order.

However, there are those who are more than happy to work in an environment where they are multitasking. This entails juggling different work activities and shifting attention from one task to another without dropping the ball. They love the adrenaline rush it gives them.

Ask yourself what 'responsibility environment' you can see yourself being more comfortable in and try to incorporate that into your career choice.

"Everyone has been made for some particular work, and the desire for that work has been put in every heart."

~ Rumi

Chapter 5: What Does Success Look Like to Me?

"There is only one success - to be able to spend your life in your own way."

~ Christopher Morley

Success has been typically measured by the amount of money, glamour, power and position one has. This way of thinking has now shifted. Think about how many stories you've heard and read about millionaires and celebrities being depressed and suicidal. This indicates that wealth and glamour isn't necessarily a sign of success to those who have it.

Success is personal and means something different to each and every person. What success means to an entrepreneur is going to look completely different from what it looks like to an employee. A neurosurgeon is going to have a far different take on what success means than a librarian. Saving someone's life is considered a successful day for a neurosurgeon. For a librarian, a successful day looks like helping people find information, suggesting books, and teaching research techniques.

Your version of success is dependant upon your values, your experiences, and your stage in life. It is about the individual goals you have at each stage of your life and the elements that allow you to feel happy. Therefore, only you can know and understand what's important to you. **Do not define what your success looks like by comparing it to what others think it should be.**

Your definition of success will most likely change a few times throughout your life, as it is a journey that happens over time.

Your journey may have many highs and lows, and can be likened to a baby learning how to walk. One successful step will lead to another successful step - with inevitable falls in between. Mistakes and setbacks are all part of everyone's life - the trick is to simply pick up, readjust, and keep your eyes on your goal.

How can you be clear on what career success means to you right now?

Understanding What's Important To You

Hands down, the most important career-planning activity you can engage in is *finding out your own definition of success*. This is incredibly important for a couple of reasons: If you don't do this, how will you know what's best for you? and how will you be able to choose a career that is worthy of who you are as a person?

"If you don't know where you're going, you won't know when you get there."

~ Alice in Wonderland

Understanding what's important to you as a person can help you align yourself with what a successful career can look like. Being clear about how you define success and having a clarity of purpose and direction will help you to reap amazing rewards.

Try not to go through life liking what's popular and disliking what's not "cool". Being okay with what you like and what you don't like is very important. Let's use a simple example: what do you think you'd like better - living near the beach or living near the mountains? The answer just depends on what you prefer. It doesn't have anything to do with one or the other being 'better', but comes down to your preference and where you would feel happier living.

The same applies for career success. One person will be happy being a doctor while someone else may be just as happy and fulfilled being a restaurant owner - both are considered successes.

Think about the following questions and write down your honest answers:

What does accomplishment, prosperity and success look like to me?

What do I value in life?

There are millions of definitions of success - from helping the world become a better place, to owning expensive cars and amazing houses, to being a role model for people.

Once you have figured out what is important *for you* personally - there is no right or wrong answer here - you will be able to focus on your vision and the goals required to make that happen.

Chapter 6: Don't Let Others Define Your Success

"Success means having the courage, the determination, and the will to become the person you believe you were meant to be."

~ George Sheehan

Unfortunately, many people spend their whole lives knowing in their gut that the situation they are in is wrong for them. However, friends, family, and society may tell them it's just fine because it's nice, safe and secure. It's what they are supposed to be happy with, and so they never do anything to change it. They may question their choices and struggle with understanding why they're not truly happy - but they stay where they are and continue to do what they do.

Instead of being one these people, allow yourself to be an individual and allow yourself to have your own vision of what success looks like to you. **It is key to attaining happiness and fulfillment.** This type of personal perspective on success is replacing the handed-down version for many people.

There is no one correct definition of career success, as it can mean different things to different individuals. Think about that - there are as many definitions of success as there are people in this world.

One person may think success is surfing all day and making money at night as a cook to pay rent and to simply get by. That might be successful for him/her at that point in time. However it's not going to be successful for someone with a wife, kids, a mortgage, and a car payment.

Different people have different perceptions of success and it doesn't mean any one is worse or better than the other.

If there are so many definitions of success out there, then which one should you pick? The one that's right for you! – not anyone else. Defining what's important to you is deeply personal and takes some soul searching. It starts with having a clear idea of how you picture success for you personally.

If you don't define what success means to you, it will be defined for you!

Through osmosis you are already seeing and following what models of career and life success are. The issue with this is that these models are other people's definitions of success, not yours.

What happens when you live other people's dreams?

The following is an example of what can happen. It is my own personal story but can strike a chord with anyone that is struggling with making others happy instead of themselves:

____

"I, along with most of my friends, were the children of immigrants. We grew up surrounded by other Greek families who either came to Canada when they were little, or who were the first in their household to be born there. My mother was a single parent, and it was just her and I living in a tiny rented apartment. She was quick to tell me that she moved across the world and sacrificed everything - for me - to give me a better life and a better chance at security, freedom, and most of all opportunity.

Let's fast forward a few years. I now worked as a secretary for a large company - my mother's dream job for me. It was everything she wanted for her daughter - I had health benefits, paid vacations, retirement contributions, a pension, and room for advancement. I had my own desk and even got to wear dresses and nice shoes in a clean and secure environment. I did not need to work three different jobs and pick through Goodwill clothes like my mother did, and I didn't have to save my pennies for years in order to buy a new living room sofa.

It was the fulfillment of her immigrant dreams for her daughter. I felt her happiness and saw her pride. I knew her dream for my security was now fulfilled - and it was absolutely suffocating me."

____

Unfortunately, you will never feel successful, fulfilled or happy if you follow a path that isn't your own - even when you achieve your goals and arrive at your destination it won't feel right. This is because you have achieved someone else's goals and arrived at someone else's destination.

Remember that **success is simply an individual goal achieved - a perception of a personal lifestyle.**

It is definitely challenging to identify goals and definitions of success that are true to you instead of ones you have inherited from your family and society. Understand that someone else's model of success may or may not work for you, even if it's taken from people who care about you.

Be aware of your assumptions of success and be bold enough to question them to see if they apply to you personally.

Chapter 7: What Are My Core Values?

"Your beliefs become your thoughts. Your thoughts become your words. Your words become your actions. Your actions become your habits. Your habits become your values. Your values become your destiny."

~ Mahatma Ghandi

You have two forms of values - personal values and core values.

Personal values are lessons you've learned from your life's trials and errors. Your core values, however, emanate from the centre of who you are. They are the things that you believe are important to you as a human being and are reflected in the way you conduct your life. They are the true representation of your authentic self.

Core values are embedded in you during your upbringing, and act as a filter for the way you act and react to life. They should determine your priorities, and deep down they are the measures you use to tell if your life is turning out the way you want it to.

Although your core values may not exactly match anyone else's, they will help you decide on what you want your surrounding culture to be like. You can use these values to select friendships, relationships, and to make career decisions.

Sadly, most of us don't know what our core values are, and our authenticity is not always presented properly to the world. We don't understand what is most important to us. We focus on what our society, family, culture, and media values instead.

This means that our values are hidden under the blanket that other people and circumstances put over them. The vast majority of people just speculate and idealize what they think they should value and what they think would make them look good to others.

Unfortunately, if you don't clearly identify, honour, and live by your core values, then your emotional, mental, and physical state will begin to suffer. This is often indicated by a nagging within, alerting you to something you should not have allowed to happen or a situation that you have participated in that was out of your 'comfort zone'.

That is why it is important for you to know and stand firm on what your values are, and just as important to live by them. You will have a greater sense of self and an understanding of how you orient to the world when your core values are clear to you. This will lead to experiencing greater fulfillment and greater alignment throughout your life.

Understanding your values and knowing what's right for you isn't simple. In fact, it's a lifetime of reassessment that requires thought and practice.

Hint: If you have no idea what your core values are, start by making a list of values and qualities that you simply can't stand. What qualities do you dislike in your friends, family, or well-known people?

Write these qualities down and then write the opposite next to them. This will help you put together a starter list of values. The next chapter will help you define your core values even further.

"If we can get to the place where we show up as our genuine selves, and let each other see who we really are, the awe-inspiring ripple effect will change the world."

~ Terrie M. Williams

Chapter 8: How Do I Define My Core Values?

"To feed what you value, to align your energy, attention, time, and resources with what you say is important to you, starts to bring your power out of hiding.

It takes courage because most people are in a cultural trance where contradiction is the norm. There is a lot of cultural validation for living a life where you feed what you don't value instead of what you do. There is a lot of validation for remaining in the trance."

~ Debrena Jackson Gandy

When the way you conduct your life matches your true values, life is usually good – you're satisfied and content. When the way you conduct your life doesn't align with your true values, that's when things start to feel wrong - and this can turn out to be a source of unhappiness.

Here are three examples of career choices with mismatched values:

- Spending quality time with your family and friends is something you really value, however you have decided on a career path that is known to be associated with overtime and weekend work. How will that career decision ultimately make you feel? Stressed? Frustrated? Resentful?

- Competition is something you really don't value, however you have decided to go into a career that has a highly competitive work environment, such as sales. How will that career decision ultimately make you feel? Overwhelmed? Anxious?

- You think innovation is one of your core values until you realize that your life thrives on stability rather than constant change. Think of how that might make you feel.

Knowing what your values are and weaving them into your career can greatly impact the level of satisfaction you can achieve. Using them as decision guidelines can help keep you true to yourself.

As your definition of success changes, so do your values. For example, when you first start your career, making money may be your top priority and may be the way you measure success. However, after you settle down and have a family, you may value work-life balance much more. It is very important to keep in touch with your values and revisit them throughout your lifetime.

Whether you recognize it or not, values already exist in your life. You just need to define what they are and how they will play a part in your life.

For example, let's say you feel that honesty may be one of your core values. What does this actually mean? How would having the core value of honesty affect your personal and career life?

Well, it can definitely lead to a far easier and fulfilled life because it allows you to be authentic and real with yourself and the people around you. It means more than telling the truth, it means being truthful about what you want and what you need in order to be happy. Honesty empowers you, it promotes openness, and also allows you to see things around you with more clarity. Your life will have far less worry if you always deal in the truth instead of excuses and lies. And you will ultimately gain your own self-respect as well as the respect of others. Honesty is without doubt one of the most admired traits of any successful, responsible person.

This is a great example of how keeping in touch with just one core value throughout your life can lead to much less frustration and indecision. This one value of honesty can allow you to live how you really feel, even if you don't always know exactly what you want.

If you have a good understanding of your values, you can be in a better position to determine what success means for you, and how best to achieve it. This is why making a conscious effort to identify your values early on is so important.

Think of yourself as a tree: your values are your roots that keep you grounded in what's important to you. The growth of your trunk, branches, leaves and fruit throughout your lifetime is determined by the strength of your roots (or values).

Most people have between five to seven core values that identify who they are. Each person's values are particular to that person. Even if two people pick the same value, such as honesty, each person will demonstrate it differently in daily actions and language.

You can get a pretty good idea of what your core values are if you take just 30 minutes out of your day and do the following exercise. Get a piece of paper and a pen and let's get started!

1. There are hundreds of core values, but only certain ones will truly resonate with you. To determine what your core values are, take a look at the list below and write down the words that feel right to you personally. Feel free to add any you don't see on this list. Don't worry about making the 'right' choice, simply jot down what you feel is important to you.

Acceptance	Dedication	Kindness	Punctuality
Abundance	Diversity	Knowledge	Professionalism
Accountability	Dependability	Leadership	Relationships
Achievement	Empathy	Love	Resilience
Advocacy	Encouragement	Learning	Reliability
Adventure	Ethics	Loyalty	Resourcefulness
Ambition	Enthusiasm	Mindfulness	Responsiveness
Appreciation	Excellence	Making a Difference	Responsibility
Autonomy	Expressiveness	Motivation	Security
Attractiveness	Family	Open-Mindedness	Self-Control
Balance	Fairness	Optimism	Selflessness
Being the Best	Friendships	Originality	Stability
Benevolence	Flexibility	Passion	Simplicity
Brilliance	Fun	Personal Development	Success
Boldness	Freedom	Performance	Teamwork
Calmness	Generosity	Proactive	Thoughtfulness
Caring	Grace	Professionalism	Thankfulness
Challenge	Growth	Quality	Traditionalism
Cheerfulness	Flexibility	Risk Taking	Trustworthiness
Charity	Happiness	Recognition	Understanding
Cleverness	Health	Safety	Usefulness
Community	Honesty	Service	Uniqueness
Compassion	Humor	Security	Vision
Commitment	Humility	Spirituality	Versatility
Cooperation	Inclusiveness	Stability	Wealth
Contribution	Individuality	Perfection	Warmth
Collaboration	Independence	Peace	Wisdom
Consistency	Innovation	Playfulness	Well-being
Curiosity	Intelligence	Power	Zeal
Creativity	Inspiration	Popularity	
Credibility	Intuition	Proactivity	
Decisiveness	Joy	Preparedness	
Daring			

2. *Take the list of core values you have just created and group all your similar values together so they personally make sense to you. Try and have no more than five different groups. See the following table for an example as to how you can do this.*

Independence	Relationships	Thankfulness	Balance	Playfulness
Peace	Compassion	Encouragement	Health	Fun
Wealth	Open-mindedness	Appreciation	Well-being	Joy
Security	Intuition	Mindfulness	Spirituality	Humor
Freedom	Love	Thoughtfulness	Personal Development	Inspiration
Abundance	Kindness			Happiness
Flexibility	Making a Difference			Optimism
Growth	Inclusiveness			Cheerfulness
	Trustworthiness			
	Acceptance			

3. Choose just one word within each of your value groups as the main word for the whole group - what you want to do is define the value that feels personally right for you. Do not overthink this step as there aren't any wrong or right answers. As you can see in the example below, the main word for each group is bolded.

Independence	Relationships	Thankfulness	Balance	Playfulness
Peace	Compassion	Encouragement	Health	Fun
Wealth	Open-mindedness	Appreciation	**Well-being**	Joy
Security	Intuition	**Mindfulness**	Spirituality	Humor
Freedom	Love	Thoughtfulness	Personal Development	Inspiration
Abundance	Kindness			**Happiness**
Flexibility	**Making a Difference**			Optimism
Growth	Inclusiveness			Cheerfulness
	Trustworthiness			
	Acceptance			

4. In order to see each of your chosen values as something actionable in your life, add a verb. Doing this exercise will help define the actions you will need to pursue in your life in order to feel like you are on the right track and living a life of purpose. This can be a very powerful exercise.

See the following as examples:

- <u>Enjoy</u> life in freedom.

- <u>Search</u> out opportunities for making a difference.

- <u>Live</u> with mindfulness.

- <u>Advocate</u> for well-being.

- <u>Exemplify</u> happiness.

5. Now write these down in the order you feel is correct for you, with the most important at the top. When faced with any decisions you have to make in your life, you can refer to these value statements and base your decisions on them. For example, your order of priority can be like the following example:

1. Enjoy life in freedom.

2. Live with mindfulness.

3. Advocate for well-being.

4. Exemplify happiness.

5. Search out opportunities for making a difference.

Now, let's just take it a little bit further. For example, if you want "happiness" to be one of your core values, ask yourself the following questions:

Why do you want to choose this particular core value?

How will your personal experiences be different if you possess this value?

What opportunities do you think you'll miss out on if you don't have this value in your life?

How will you make this core value become a part of the way you think and behave? What actions do you think you'll need to take to incorporate this value?

What do you think this value will mean in your life? What will it bring to your life?

If you go through this exercise for each of your most important core values, you'll have an incredible resource that you'll always be able to refer to.

Knowing what your core values are can help to guide and lead you when making decisions, not only for your career but for your life as well. It is one of the most important things to know about yourself, and unfortunately it isn't something that is taught in school.

Simply determine if the choices you make in life line up with your core values. Every now and then, ask yourself; "How well did my decisions and behaviour today align with my values?" If your life lines up with what you value, it will be purpose-filled and happy.

Now that you have defined what your core values are, acknowledge them and **make plans and decisions that honour them**.

If you keep them in mind as you journey through life, you will have clear direction and be quick and focused when making decisions.

Note: If you plan on becoming a leader one day in your place of work, leading with your core values is crucial. This is because it creates and keeps company culture, makes it easier to hire and fire employees, guides the direction that the company will go in, and adds worth and meaning to the work. That meaning starts with the leader and his or her own core values, and is then passed down to the rest of the employees.

"To be yourself in a world that is constantly trying to make you something else is the greatest accomplishment."

~ Ralph Waldo Emerson

Chapter 9: Slaying The Fear of Failure

Failure - An instance or act of being unsuccessful or failing

Fear - To be fearful, afraid, apprehensive, to dread, to be terrified

---

We *all* fail in life, it's just part of life and part of learning.

We all have our own definition of failure. This is based on what our core values are as well as what our belief system is. One person's failure might simply be a challenge to someone else.

Failure is a stumbling block, a learning experience, or a temporary set-back - *until you couple it with fear.*

Most people have likely experienced a fear of failure at one time or another. Perhaps subconsciously you have sabotaged your own progress in order to avoid the possibility of failure - or because you are secretly afraid of looking like a failure to friends and family.

Ask yourself the following questions and see if you can identify with any of them:

Am I reluctant to try new things?

Do I procrastinate a lot?

Do I have low self-confidence, low self-esteem, and self-doubt?

Do I have a passion I wish I could pursue but talk myself out of it?

Am I a perfectionist? Do I only want to do things that I know I'm good at?

Think of the determination that a baby must have when learning how to walk. He or she endures many tumbles and falls before mastering the art of putting one foot in front of the other. All of us were babies and young children at one time, and we all had the same fearless determination to learn how to walk, how to run, how to talk, and how to adapt to our surroundings. We weren't deterred by a fear of failing - we simply tried again and again until we learned what to do and what not to do in order to succeed.

Why then, are we so afraid and hesitant to make mistakes in our adult lives? Why are we afraid to fail if it leads to us learning a new skill? What happened to our childhood determination? Try going down 'Memory Lane' for a bit and think of times when fear wasn't an option and trying new things was just fun.

Where Does Fear of Failure Come From?

As we get older, self-doubt creeps in, our inner critic becomes stronger and our positive self-talk begins to fade. We begin to doubt who we are, what we believe, and whether we have the ability to make things happen.

Allowing fear - *for only we can allow fear to control what we do* - can make us become so cautious in our decision-making that we may miss out on amazing opportunities. A fear of failure can be numbing and paralyzing. It can cause us to completely stop any forward motion in our life and can blind us to seeing any opportunities that come our way.

Fear of failure can come to us in a variety of ways. Here are two of the most common:

- **Our parents were very unsupportive and critical when we were growing up.** It is very common that people who are motivated by the fear of failure tend to have had parents who very rarely praised their successes, and instead readily punished their failures. Many people carry a multitude of insecurities and negative feelings into their adulthood from childhood trauma.

- **We extended a lot of effort at one point in our lives but still failed.** This, therefore, implied to us that we had low ability and therefore, low worth. The conclusion we came to was that if we didn't put forth any effort into anything and still failed, this wouldn't reflect negatively on our ability - our worth would still remain intact. We have given up on trying to succeed, and any success that we do experience we immediately attribute to circumstances outside of our control.

How can some people get over failure after failure and achieve success?

How can they turn huge setbacks into things that not only positively affect themselves but the whole world?

It's simply this - *they don't let their circumstances or misfortunes dictate their attitude.*

Choosing Our Perception and Reaction

The amazing thing about having failures and setbacks is that **we can choose how we perceive them - and most importantly, how we react to them.**

The following are some common thoughts and reactions people have when faced with failure:

- failure is solid proof of how inadequate I am; others were right about me

- failure is a good way out and an excuse for me to move on to something safer

- failure is an important lesson and a chance for me to improve and grow

- failure is a reminder for me not to make that same mistake again

When confronted with failure, we can question our overall skills and abilities, *or* we can treat it as a specific instance that doesn't say anything at all about our skills. If you don't take failure personally and consider it as a stone on your path, then you can kick that stone out of your way and continue on.

If there is a skill you want to learn or a career you want to pursue, go for it. You'll probably fail at first and that's a great thing - you'll soon start to associate your failures with progress. Don't be embarrassed or afraid to fail. Instead, embrace the failure and learn how strong and resilient you can be.

"Inaction breeds doubt and fear. Action breeds confidence and courage. If you want to conquer fear, do not sit home and think about it. Go out and get busy."

Dale Carnegie

Shedding Light On Your Belief System

When it comes to your career, what you believe about yourself plays an enormous part in determining how successful you will be. Success isn't just about how competent or capable you are; it's also about what you believe is possible and what you believe you are worthy of doing.

Our belief system is always running in the background of our mind, much like an operating system does on a personal computer. This operating system contains many files - everything we 'believe' to be true about other people, the world around us, and about ourselves. These are our 'truths' and we 100% believe them to be factual, so much so that we experience everything in our lives through the lens of these 'truths'.

So, where do these truths/beliefs come from? They mainly come from the things you heard and experienced as a child. Your young subconscious mind was similar to a sponge; it soaked up all the messages it heard and accepted them as truths without questioning them. Your self-image was completely formed by what you were told by your parents, grandparents, relatives and friends, and also by what situations you were put in.

If you heard statements like 'you are so lazy' or 'you are never going to amount to anything', you had no reason to doubt those statements were true since your cognitive ability to reason didn't start maturing until you were a teenager. You saved those limiting beliefs much like files saved in a computer, and they have been running on 'auto-pilot' ever since.

Just as a virus can slow down or completely disable your computer's operating system, so can limiting beliefs slow down or disable your ability to get things done or become successful.

What's important to remember is that you are no longer that young child. Your cognitive ability has since matured and has the ability to reason and understand. You now have the ability to see that other people's opinions were just that; their own opinions. Perhaps they said things out of frustration, out of anger, or out of their own immaturity. Whatever the case, these do not need to be your truths anymore.

Take a few minutes to make a list of what you think your negative beliefs are. Being aware of them is the first important step to understanding your limitations. Ask yourself where the root of each belief has come from. Looking back, was the person that made the statement struggling with their own life and perhaps had their own issues to deal with? Maybe they took it out on you and had no idea how their words and actions would affect your life later on.

Beside each negative belief you've written down, write down as many examples as you can of things that you have done in your life that are the complete opposite to that statement. For example, if one of your negative beliefs is that you are lazy, write down all the things that you have accomplished in your life that prove otherwise. By doing this exercise and acknowledging your achievements, your contaminated files in your subconscious mind will gradually be tossed out and replaced with healthy ones.

Note: Your subconscious mind is very reluctant to get rid of one of its 'files' unless it is replaced with another. Therefore, it is very important for you to be diligent in reinforcing positive thoughts about yourself so that your belief system will be updated with a truer representation of who you are.

"It is important to our healing that we sort out the belief systems we adopt; belief systems that were taught to us and because they are so full of lies, they lead to all kinds of depressions, addictions and other struggles while we try to cope with the manifestations of the problems instead of the roots of the problems."

— Darlene Ouimet

Our reaction to failure and our belief in our abilities will make all the difference in how fast we reach success, both in our career choice and in our life. Adopt an attitude of gratitude and program (or reprogram) your life to be grateful for everything in your life, even the failures. And certainly don't let a negative or fearful belief be the reason why you stay in an idle state for the rest of your life and why you never reach your potential.

Chapter 10: What Will My 'Word' Be?

"Yeah, we're always talking about following your passion, but we're all part of the flow of history ... you've got to put something back into the flow of history that's going to help your community, help other people ... so that 20, 30, 40 years from now ... people will say, this person didn't just have a passion, he cared about making something that other people could benefit from."

~ Steve Jobs

What does the word **'work'** mean?

Typically, it implies something you have to do, or something that may be hard to do. If you have to work eight hours a day, you probably don't find it very exciting or fulfilling. It is a means to a paycheque.

What does the word **'career'** mean?

This word most likely feels like it has a bigger meaning than the word 'work'. It implies something you don't mind putting some effort and energy into because it has some purpose - it is "an occupation undertaken for a significant period of a person's life with opportunities for progress".

What does the word **'passion'** mean?

This word is quite powerful, and can conjure up an image of someone putting far more energy into something than is normally required because they are passionate about it. It is often associated with ambition that is materialized into action and has a lot of heart, mind, body and soul behind it. It has the ability to shake your mind free from old patterns of thinking and from limiting beliefs.

What does the word **'mission'** mean?

This word is very large, it is expansive. It typically means involvement in something that is associated with a higher purpose, something that positively impacts the world. Someone who is 'on a mission' or who 'has a mission' usually doesn't consider what they are doing as being work at all.

What happens when you combine the words **passion and mission**?

Having passion for something that is coupled with a mission isn't just having a goal or having the willpower to see something through. It is a driving force that gives you a sense of purpose - it is strong, compelling, and all-encompassing. **It is a hunger and a calling, not a career.**

"You must find something you want to live for that's bigger than yourself—a mission—whether it's your children, a business, a non-profit, whatever. That pulls you to achieve, which is far more sustainable than to push yourself to. You can only push yourself for so long."

~ Tony Robbins

____

Ask yourself the following:

What do you believe your passion or your mission is? What is your purpose for being here on this earth?

Never mind what you or others 'think' you should be.

Instead, what do you want to create or to give to others? What could you do every single day and not get sick of it? What is your gift, or your light, that you want to share with the world? What do you want to do better than others? How can you make a difference to the people around you or to the world?

We all have a purpose, whether we know what it is or not. If you continuously ask yourself these questions throughout the various stages of your life, you will discover the meaning of passion in reference to YOU.

Your answers may or may not change over time as you mature and grow. However, asking yourself these questions throughout your life will keep you on track and will help you be true to yourself and your purpose.

Don't think that you have to be the next Bill or Melinda Gates or the next Oprah Winfrey to make a difference. There are many everyday, ordinary people who have found their special niche in which they have contributed at their highest level. They aren't all privileged, advantaged or special either. Many have come from very difficult and disadvantaged circumstances and have started with limited capabilities.

The difference is that they have found their purpose, their 'light', and have managed to pick themselves up and rise above their circumstances. Their passion or mission has woken them up to something in life that they hunger for so strongly that they no longer have to push themselves to do anything. They have discovered a different kind of drive; a force that pulls them forward.

Sadly, the majority of people in our society spend their time at *work* to make ends meet. They also end up spending more time working than they do with their family. They have either never had the opportunity or the awareness to tap into their own gifts and use them to make a difference. They have not allowed themselves to be more - to work for a higher purpose than just making an income.

There are also many people that don't allow themselves to find or experience purpose in their lives because they don't want to be disappointed. These people think that by moderating their joy levels they are holding off feeling sad or disappointed. However, what they're really doing is sacrificing their joy and resigning themselves to a constant state of disconnection. That feeling of being safe and certain to avoid disappointment will only succeed in closing them off to opportunities and possibilities.

It is essential to remember that staying open to uncertainty and being true to yourself offers far greater benefits than being safe and being merely a shadow of yourself.

It may be frightening to face your fears of worthiness, but it is far more empowering than choosing to sacrifice who you really are. One of the most courageous acts you can take in life might be to simply be yourself.

By reading this book, it is obvious you are taking the time to think about what path you'd like to take in your life. Everyone comes to this world to fulfill their own particular mission. For some, it may be devoting themselves to their family and being amazing parents. Others may want to share their talent for music or art in order to inspire and encourage people.

Whatever it is that you were born for, it should be focused on your own personal values. Today's modern society is losing that connection and forgetting the things that matter for the sake of material things and superficial aspirations.

"Your purpose in life is to find your purpose and give your whole heart and soul to it."

— *Gautama Buddha*

Chapter 11: What Will My Legacy Be?

"Carve your name on hearts, not tombstones. A legacy is etched into the minds of others and the stories they share about you."

~ Shannon L. Alder

You don't hear many people having conversations about leaving a legacy these days. There are a few reasons why this may be so.

One reason may be because the society we live in today is very present-minded and has very little understanding of history and time. We think that our society is the only one that really matters, and so we don't acknowledge the legacy that was handed down to us. Therefore, we don't see or even think about the benefit in leaving a legacy ourselves.

We also live in a very impatient society that wants things done right away and wants feedback for any accomplishments that are made. Building and manifesting a legacy takes a long time, and our efforts may not come to fruition and may not be recognized until after we pass away. The thought of this may not seem too appealing.

Also, because we live in a disposable society where every advancement that is made is quickly replaced by an even better version, it is easy to believe that nothing can truly be lasting. It's easy to feel that there's no point in contributing to the world if what we give is going to become obsolete anyways.

However, if you just take a minute to honour and think about the people who have left a legacy for you to follow, it may awaken something inside you to want to do the same. These are the people you know and knew, the people who have shaped your life profoundly, for better or for worse. These people can be your parents, grandparents, extended family, friends, teachers, coaches, and of course people in history whose achievements, principles, and philosophies have impacted generations.

People often think of a legacy as leaving behind material possessions or money. But a legacy isn't always about things. In fact, it's more about who you are and how you touch people's lives. There are those whose passion/legacy can end up altering the way things are done in this world, and those who inspire others and move people to become better people. Everyone leaves behind a legacy when they die, whether it's a positive one or a negative one.

For example, parents can leave their children a legacy of love and respect. Adolf Hitler left a legacy of pain and suffering. Martin Luther King Jr. left a legacy of hope and encouragement for us to keep pursuing the dream of racial equality.

There are hundreds of thousands of men and women who live and have lived in a way that affects our lives today. A legacy can come from an idea, from a business, or from someone's love and compassion. Anything that affects one person or the entire world, even just a little bit, matters.

Think about how you'd like to leave your lasting footprint on this earth - give yourself some time to think about it. Your answer to this question can ultimately steer your entire life.

Do you want to have contributed towards a safer or cleaner planet? Do you want to have spent your life helping people and making their lives better? Do you picture yourself having worked with children, the elderly, the sick, or those in distress?

By wanting to leave a positive mark and by wanting to create an example for others to follow, **a legacy can be a current pathway that can guide you in your life's decisions as to what to do and what not to do in your life.**

Try thinking about it in this way: your passion in life will ultimately become your legacy. Your decision to pursue the interests and ideas that make a difference in your life and that make you happy currently will ultimately end up influencing others in the future.

Touching people's lives in a positive way and being able to live your own unique life with purpose is key to living a happy and fulfilled life.

____

Take a few minutes to do the following exercise:

Figure out what you would like to accomplish in your life by pretending you are now at the end of your life and you are looking back. Try picturing your 85th birthday celebration, where everyone you've had an impact on has gathered together. As these people get up to say a few words about you, what would you like them to say? What you would like to hear is exactly what you want your life to stand for.

Ask yourself these questions to help you become clear on the type of legacy you wish to leave (write down your answers):

How do I want my family and friends to remember me?

How do I want those beyond my circle of family and friends to remember me?

Whose lives will I have impacted and influenced?

Do I want to leave an impact on my community, and if so, what kind of impact?

If I had to give everything I own to a cause, what cause would it be?

How can I contribute to the field I choose to go into?

What would I like my life to stand for?

How will I make the world a better place because I am in it?

Are there any lessons that I can pass on to future generations?

Remember, material possessions do not make a true legacy. It's not the things we leave FOR others that matters, it's what we leave INSIDE their hearts and minds that matters the most. Leave the world the best and most worthy parts of yourself. Today, tomorrow, and every single day thereafter, create your legacy. That's what the world really needs.

"To leave the world a bit better, whether by a healthy child, a garden patch, or a redeemed social condition; To know even one life has breathed easier because you have lived. This is to have succeeded."

– Ralph Waldo Emerson

Chapter 12: Don't Get Too Comfortable

"A ship is safe in harbor, but that's not what ships are for."

~ William G.T. Shedd

Life is very interesting; it seems to always present us with 'either-or' choices. Do we want to go this way or that way, do we want to expand or contract, do we want to climb or would we rather stay where we are?

Remember this: The entire world is at your fingertips and yours for the taking, but **only if you're hungry for it.** If you're not all that hungry, then you'll end up making safe choices. And you'll end up becoming comfortable.

The reason why a lot of people have trouble staying on one particular path is that they aren't pursuing something that resonates with their values. They end up taking two steps forward and three steps back, until they eventually fall and start all over again with something completely different. They don't commit 100% to anything, which just means there's more room to fail.

They live in a world of perpetual false starts.

The majority of people are afraid of failure (or are afraid of looking like a failure), and prefer to know they have a soft place to land if things don't turn out the way they plan. Whether their safety net is living in their parents home, having a decent-paying job with benefits, or living in a comfortable hometown where they know everyone – there's an incredible amount of comfort and certainty there.

However, what may look like a stable and encouraging home base can end up being a 'personal development prison'. It can become paralyzing and debilitating to one's growth as a human being. It can keep the 'light' buried deep within.

There is nothing like necessity to get a person through a difficult time. But nothing will ever seem really necessary until you are pursuing your passion or your mission.

Passion without hunger means that you aren't making the jump fully and you're not committing - you're holding back. However, passion coupled with hunger will pull you forward when everybody else is feeling defeated and taking a break.

Find your true passion by committing and immersing yourself into something you have an interest in. Don't just dabble in it - put your whole heart in it.

Read, learn, and commit to the process of learning everything you can. Ask questions, volunteer, and model yourself around people that have been successful in that area. Feel where that focus takes you and where it can lead you.

Know what you don't want to do, the kind of people you don't want to be around, the environment you don't want to work in. Knowing what you don't want is just as important as knowing what you do want.

Once you've narrowed in on something and you've got a hunger to pursue it, you must do one more thing to be successful and great at it:

You must figure out how this passion of yours can be of value. You must find out how it can serve other people. It cannot be about what you can get out of it, but what value others can get out of it. Understanding this point is key, so you may want to read this paragraph a few times until it fully resonates with you.

Perhaps a better way to think of it, is instead of 'following your passion', you should 'follow what's of value'.

There is nothing wrong with wanting to be great and successful, but the only people that are truly great and successful are the ones that have provided value and served other people. It's a feeling of responsibility truly successful people all seem to share; a sense of purpose that they are put here to serve.

We are living in an era of fast and furious innovation the likes of which the world has never seen. Our greatest opportunities are now global. We need to create a world where everyone has a sense of purpose. No one grows professionally and personally all by themselves. Surround yourself with like-minded people that also have a purpose, and that also want to give and not just take.

We can be the generation that ends disease, ends hunger, and helps to stop climate change. Our greatest challenges need global responses, and no one country can do everything by themselves. Progress now requires unification, not just as cities or nations, but also as a global community.

Find your passion, your mission. And pursue it with a sense of purpose and urgency.

"Purpose is that feeling that you are part of something bigger than yourself, that you are needed, and that you have something better ahead. Purpose is what creates true happiness."

~ Mark Zuckerberg